GRAPHIC LIBRARY

GRAPHIC SCIENCE

UNDERSTANDING GLOBAL WARMING

WITH MAX AXIOM SUPER SCIENTIST

An Augmented Reading Science Experience

by Agnieszka Biskup | illustrated by Cynthia Martin and Bill Anderson

Consultant:
Joseph M. Moran, PhD
Associate Director, Education Program
American Meteorological Society, Washington, D.C.

CAPSTONE PRESS
a capstone imprint

Graphic Library is published by Capstone Press,
1710 Roe Crest Drive, North Mankato, Minnesota 56003.
www.mycapstone.com

Library of Congress Cataloging-in-Publication Data is available on the Library of
Congress website.
ISBN: 978-1-5435-2953-1 (library binding)
ISBN: 978-1-5435-2964-7 (paperback)
ISBN: 978-1-5435-2974-6 (eBook PDF)

Summary: In graphic novel format, follows the adventures of Max Axiom as he
explains the science behind global warming.

Art Director and Designer
Bob Lentz and Thomas Emery

Colorist
Matt Webb

Cover Artist
Tod Smith

Editor
Donald Lemke

Photo Credits
Capstone Studio/Karon Dubke: 29; NASA: 15; Shutterstock/
Margaud: 21

Download the Capstone app!

- Ask an adult to download the Capstone 4D app.

- Scan the cover and stars inside the book for additional content.

When you scan a spread, you'll find fun extra stuff
to go with this book! You can also find these things
on the web at www.capstone4D.com using the
password: global.29531

Printed in the United States of America.
PA017

TABLE OF CONTENTS

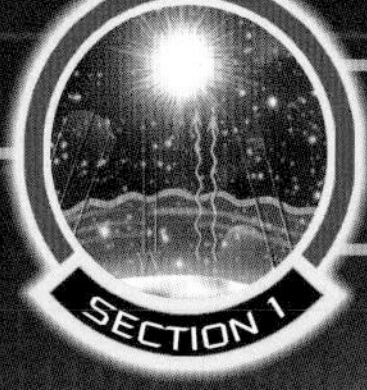
SECTION 1

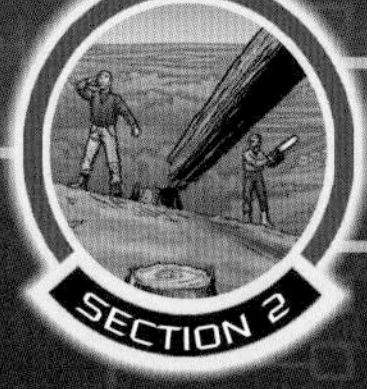
SECTION 2

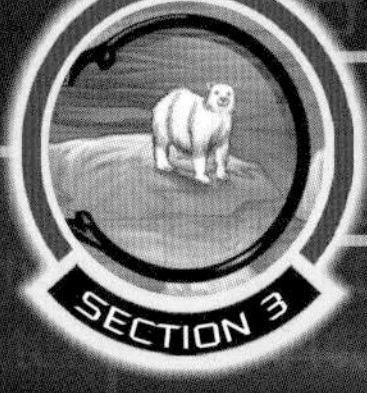
SECTION 3

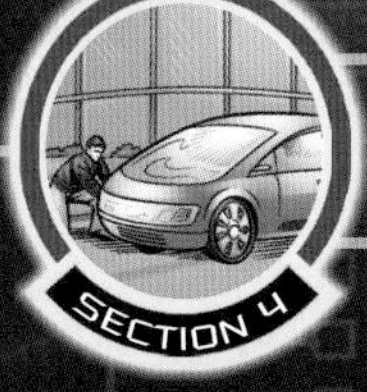
SECTION 4

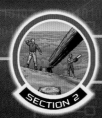

THE GREENHOUSE EFFECT

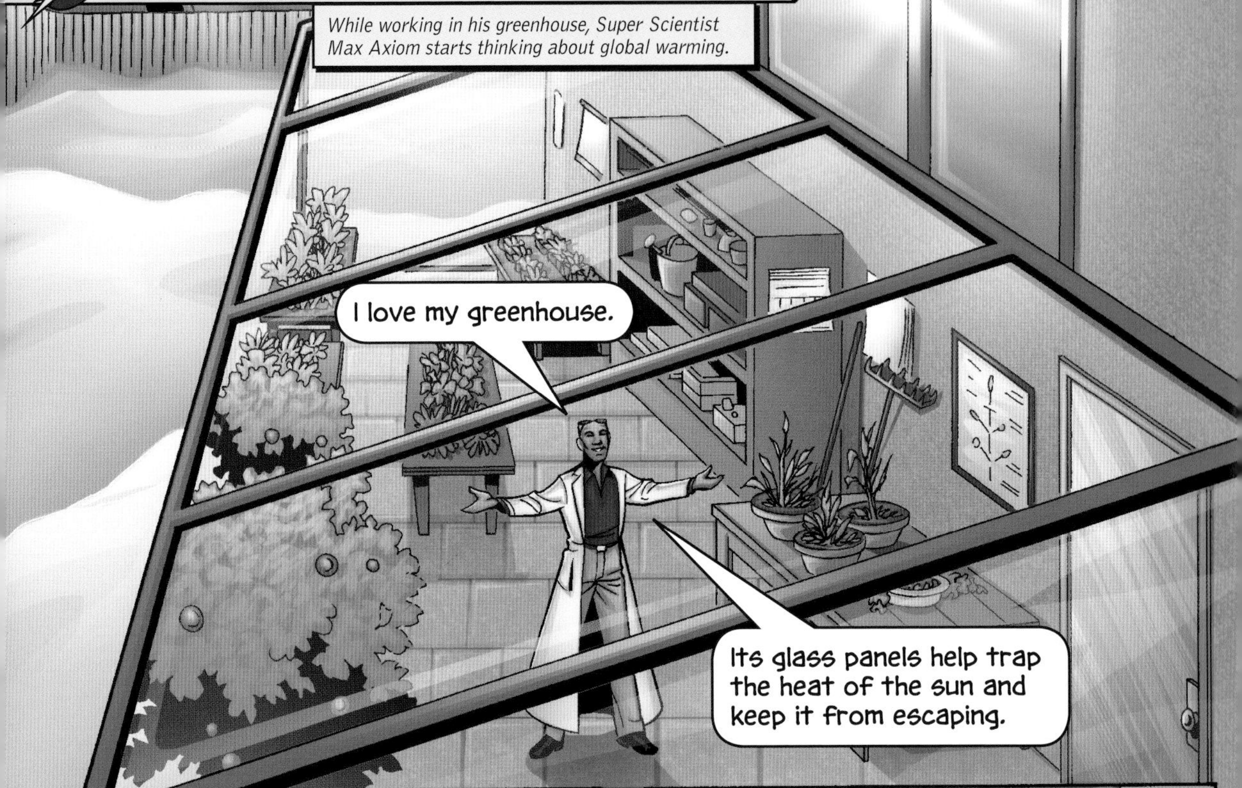
While working in his greenhouse, Super Scientist Max Axiom starts thinking about global warming.
I love my greenhouse.
Its glass panels help trap the heat of the sun and keep it from escaping.

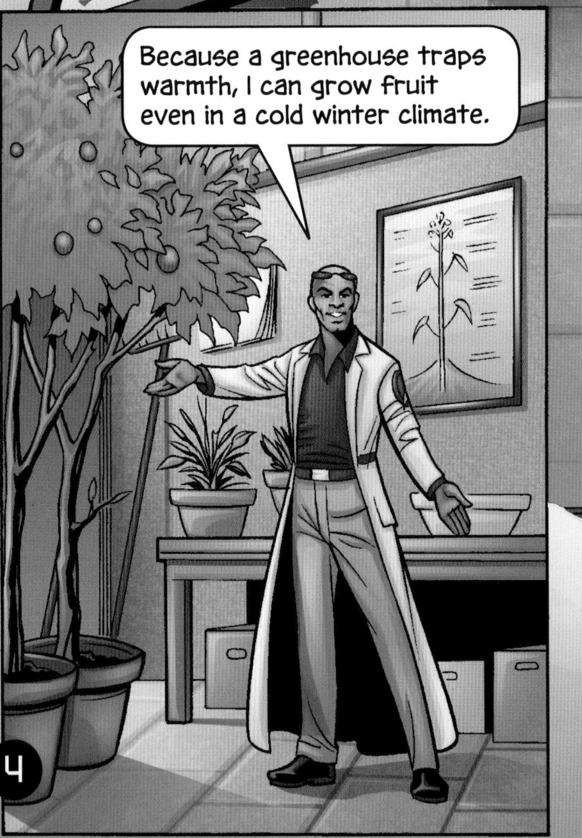
Because a greenhouse traps warmth, I can grow fruit even in a cold winter climate.

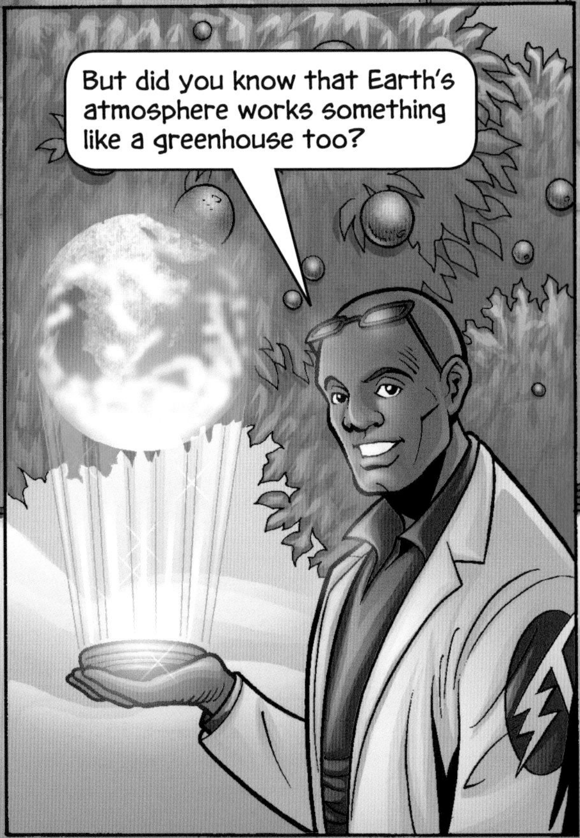
But did you know that Earth's atmosphere works something like a greenhouse too?

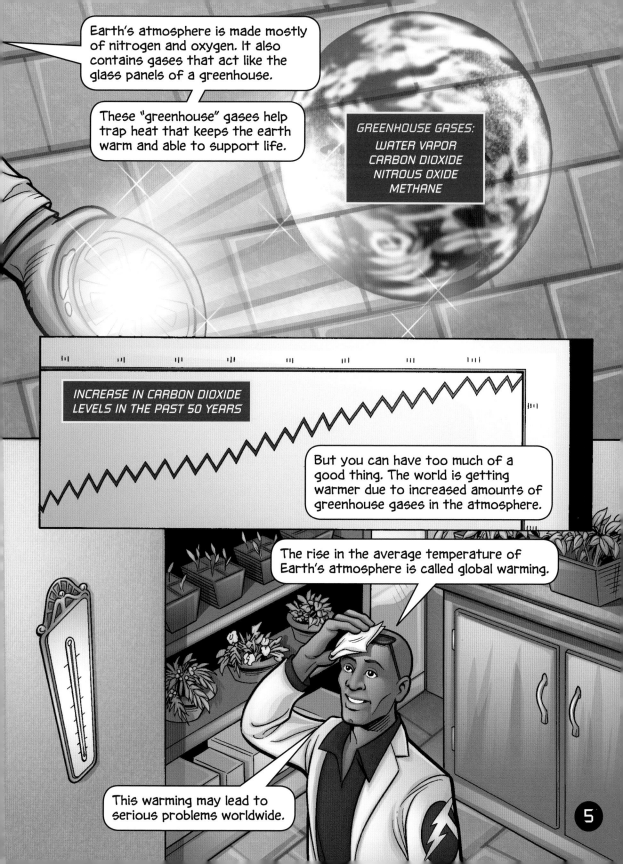

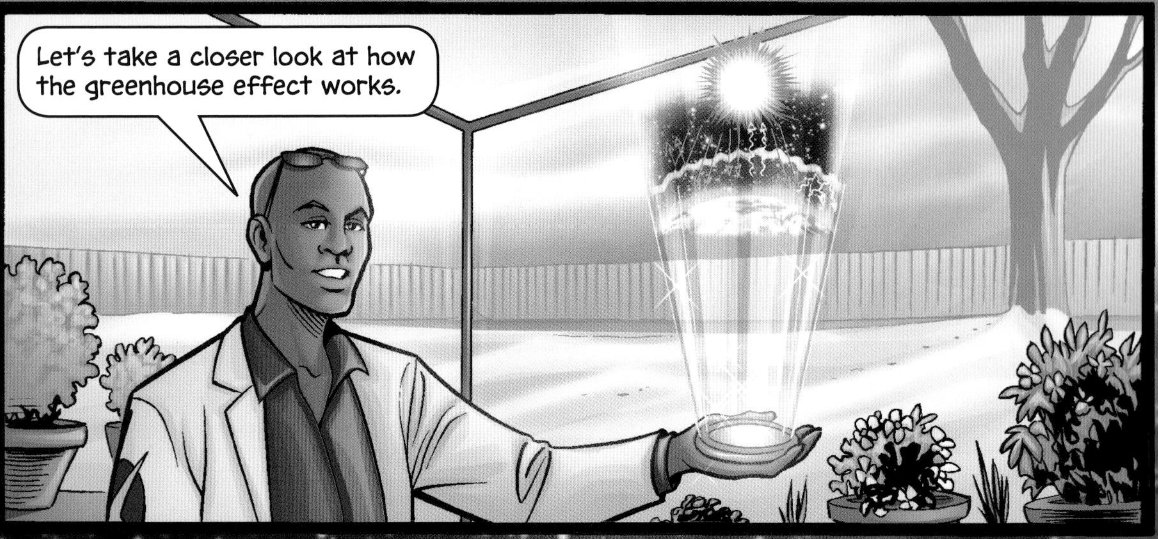
Let's take a closer look at how the greenhouse effect works.

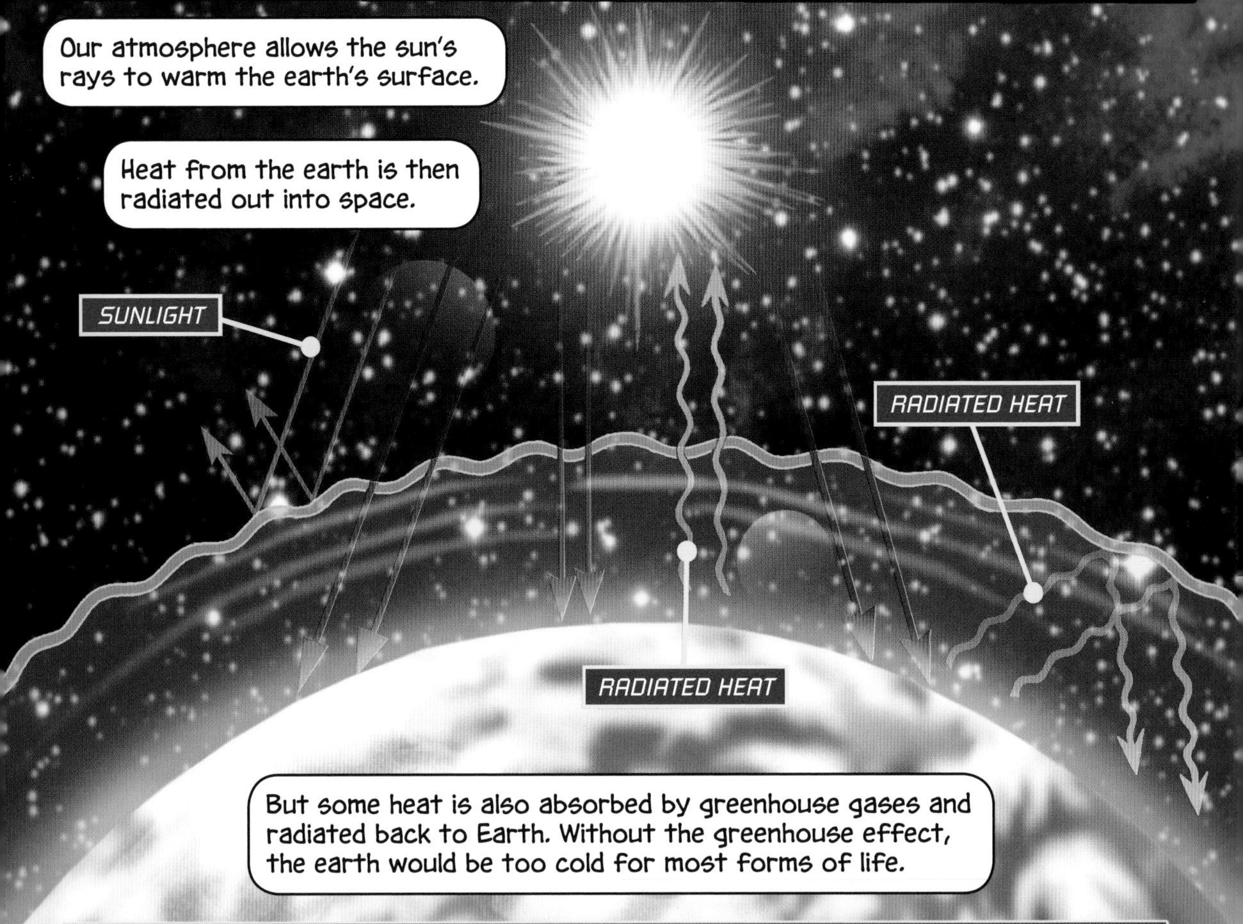
Our atmosphere allows the sun's rays to warm the earth's surface.
Heat from the earth is then radiated out into space.
SUNLIGHT
RADIATED HEAT
RADIATED HEAT
But some heat is also absorbed by greenhouse gases and radiated back to Earth. Without the greenhouse effect, the earth would be too cold for most forms of life.

HOT AND COLD MOON

The moon has no atmosphere. Its equator is a blistering 260 degrees Fahrenheit (127 degrees Celsius) in daylight. In darkness the temperature drops to a frigid minus 280 degrees Fahrenheit (minus 173 degrees Celsius).

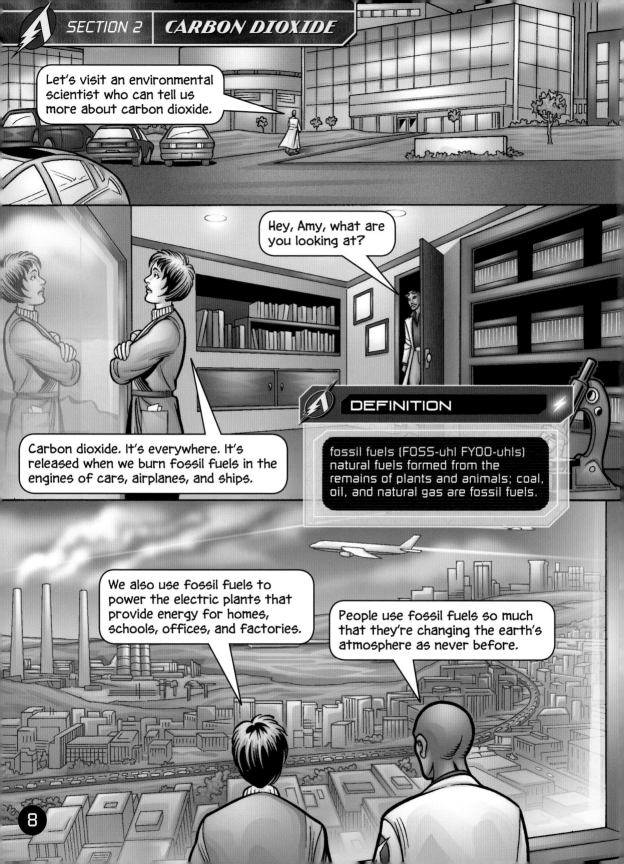

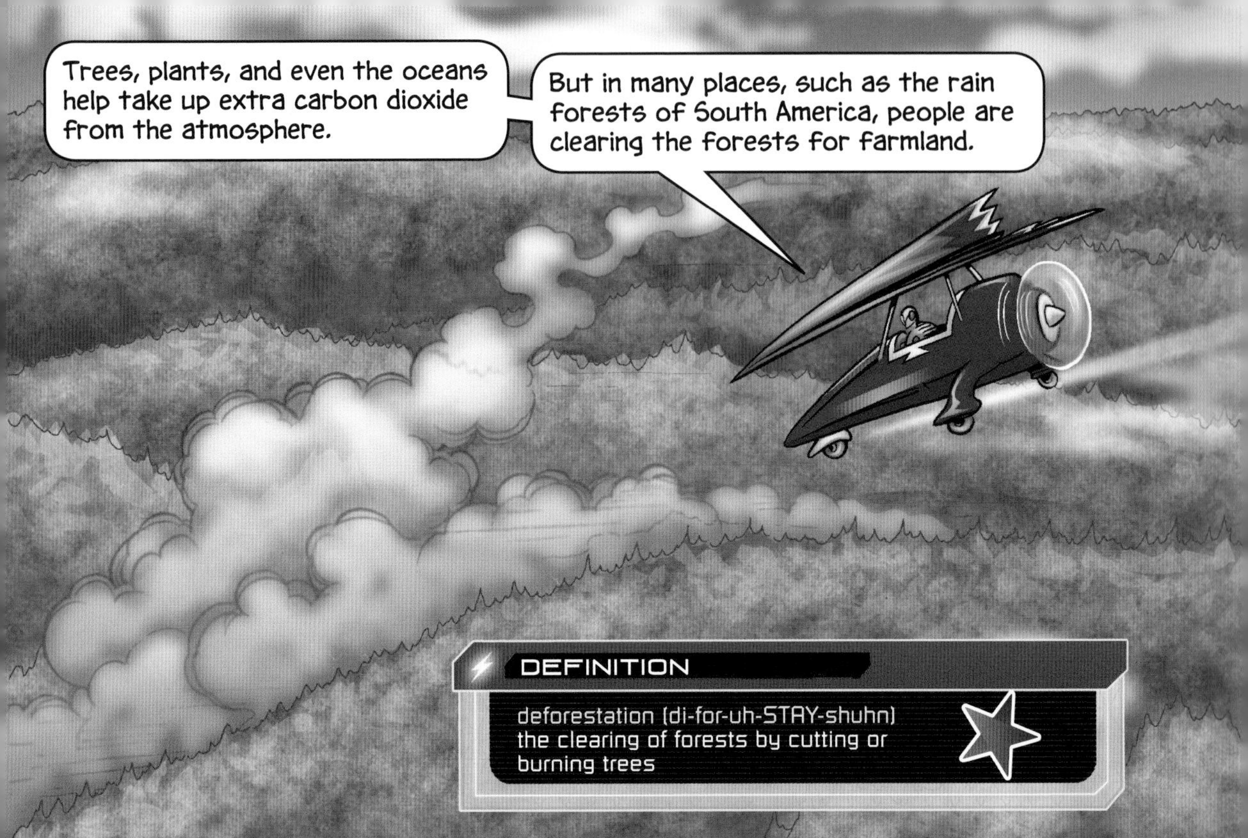

Trees, plants, and even the oceans help take up extra carbon dioxide from the atmosphere.
But in many places, such as the rain forests of South America, people are clearing the forests for farmland.

DEFINITION

deforestation (di-for-uh-STAY-shuhn) the clearing of forests by cutting or burning trees

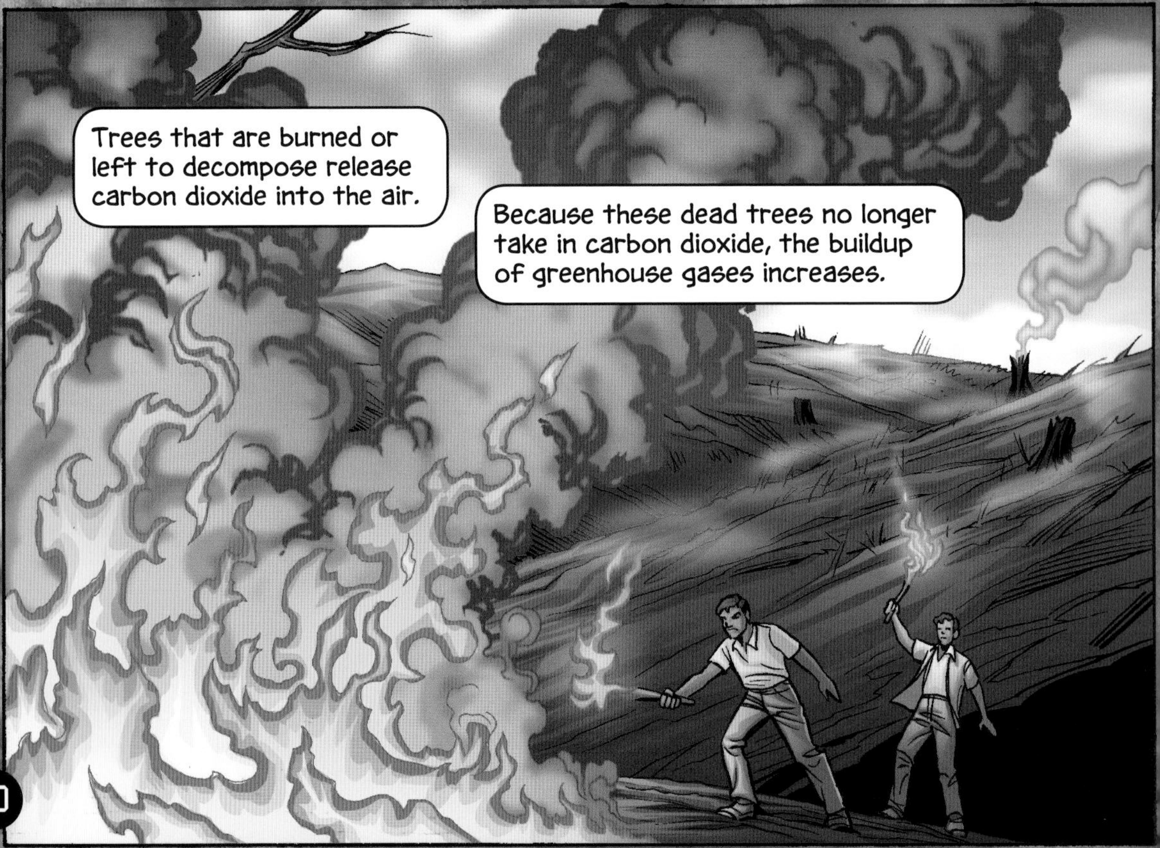

Trees that are burned or left to decompose release carbon dioxide into the air.
Because these dead trees no longer take in carbon dioxide, the buildup of greenhouse gases increases.

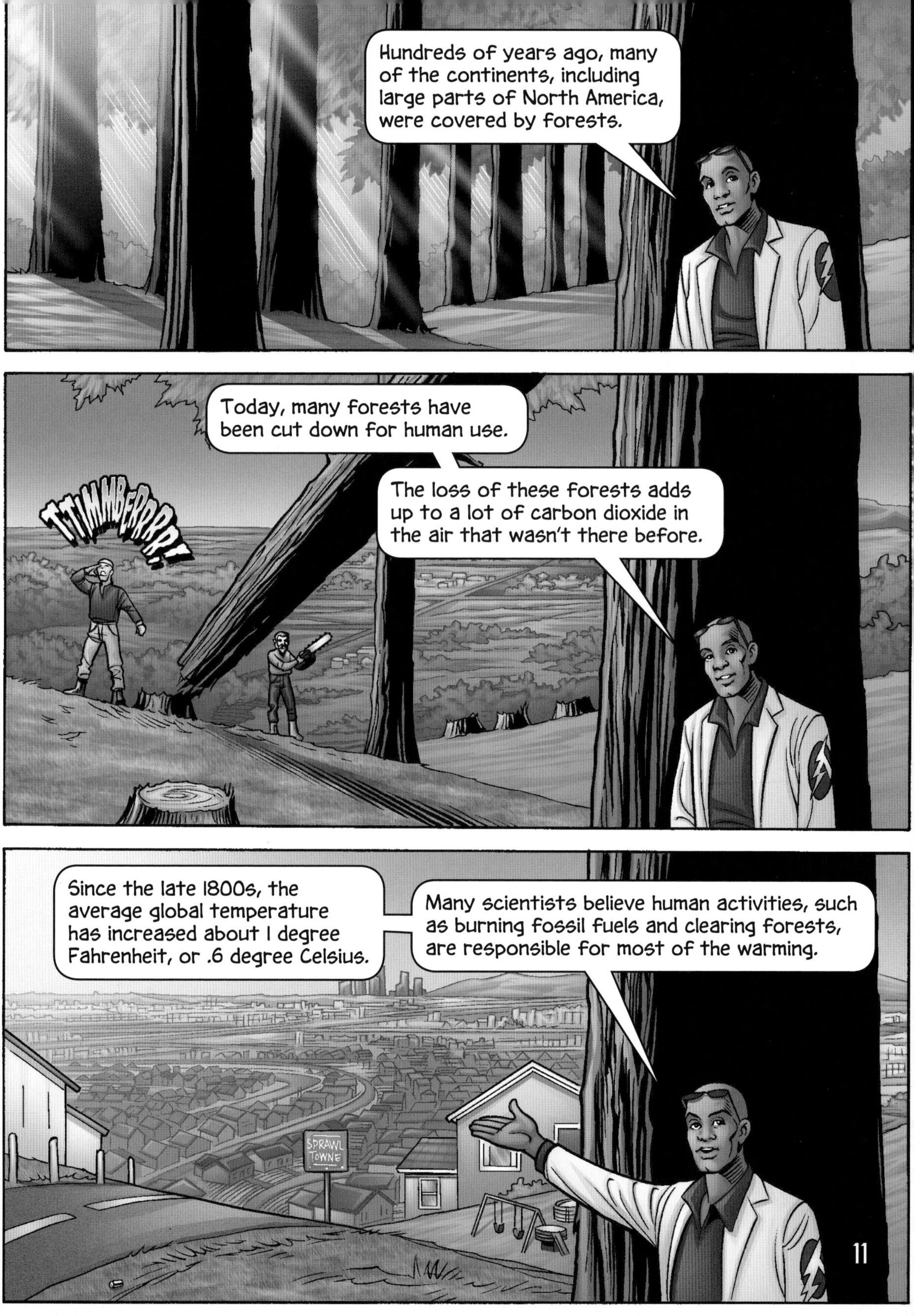
Hundreds of years ago, many of the continents, including large parts of North America, were covered by forests.
Today, many forests have been cut down for human use.
TTIMMBERRRR!
The loss of these forests adds up to a lot of carbon dioxide in the air that wasn't there before.
Since the late 1800s, the average global temperature has increased about 1 degree Fahrenheit, or .6 degree Celsius.
Many scientists believe human activities, such as burning fossil fuels and clearing forests, are responsible for most of the warming.
SPRAWL TOWNE

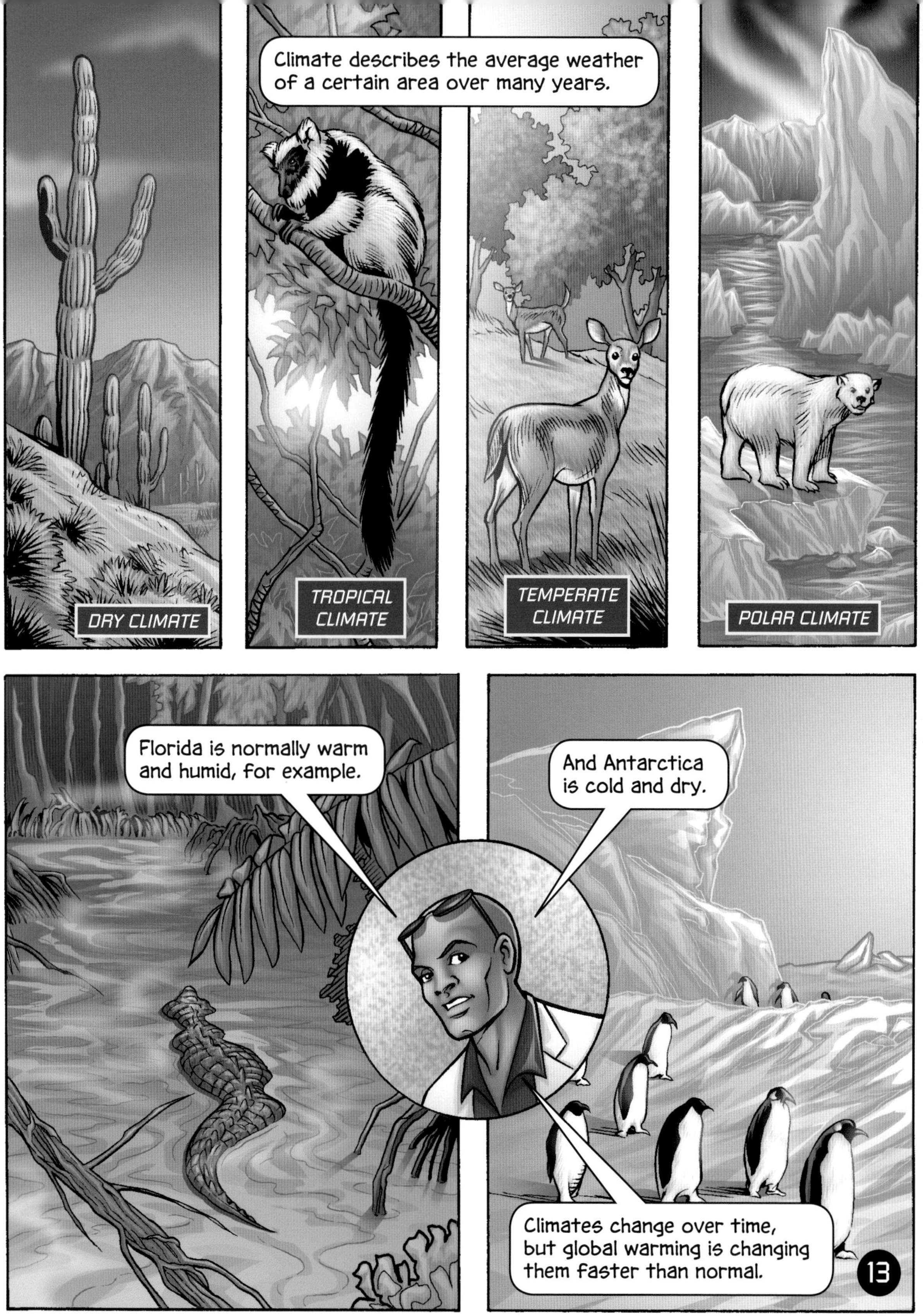
Climate describes the average weather of a certain area over many years.
DRY CLIMATE
TROPICAL CLIMATE
TEMPERATE CLIMATE
POLAR CLIMATE
Florida is normally warm and humid, for example.
And Antarctica is cold and dry.
Climates change over time, but global warming is changing them faster than normal.
13

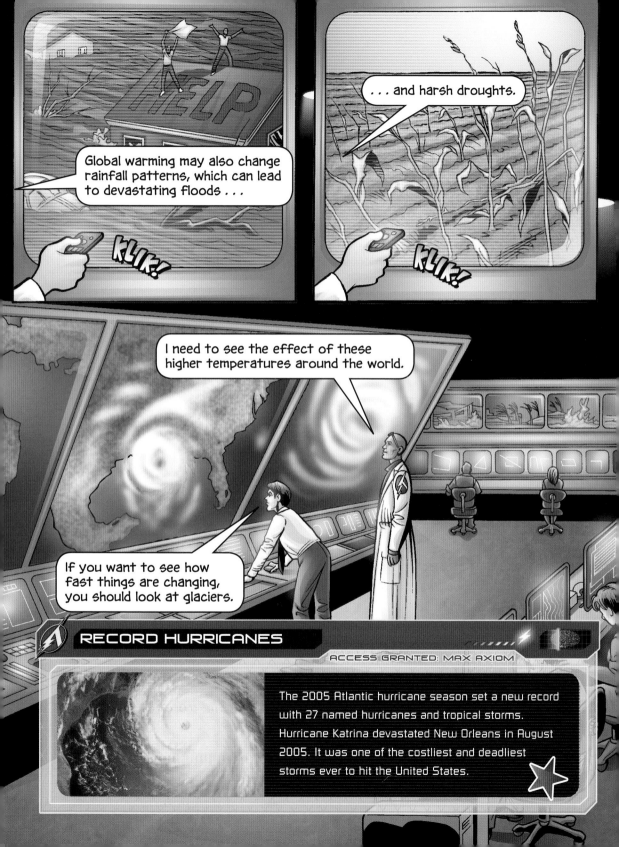

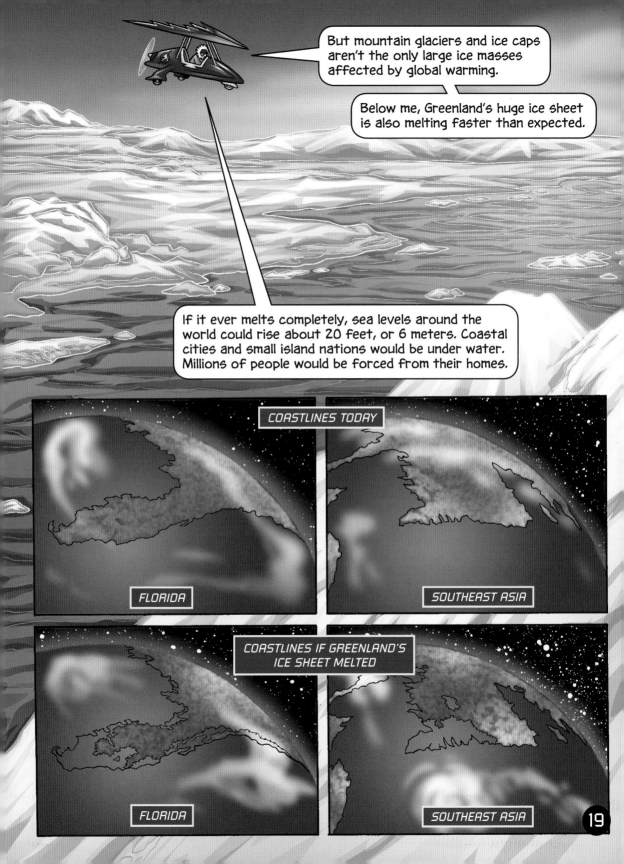

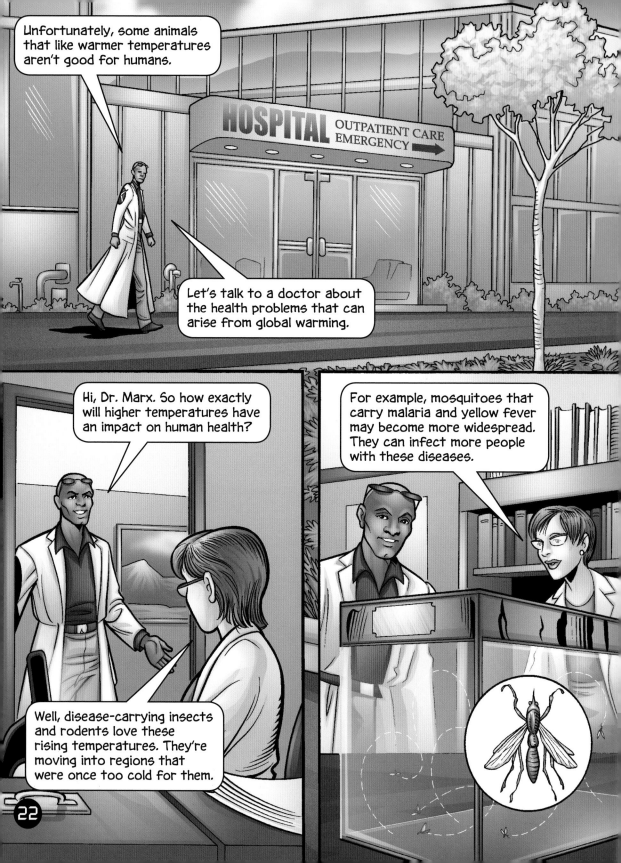

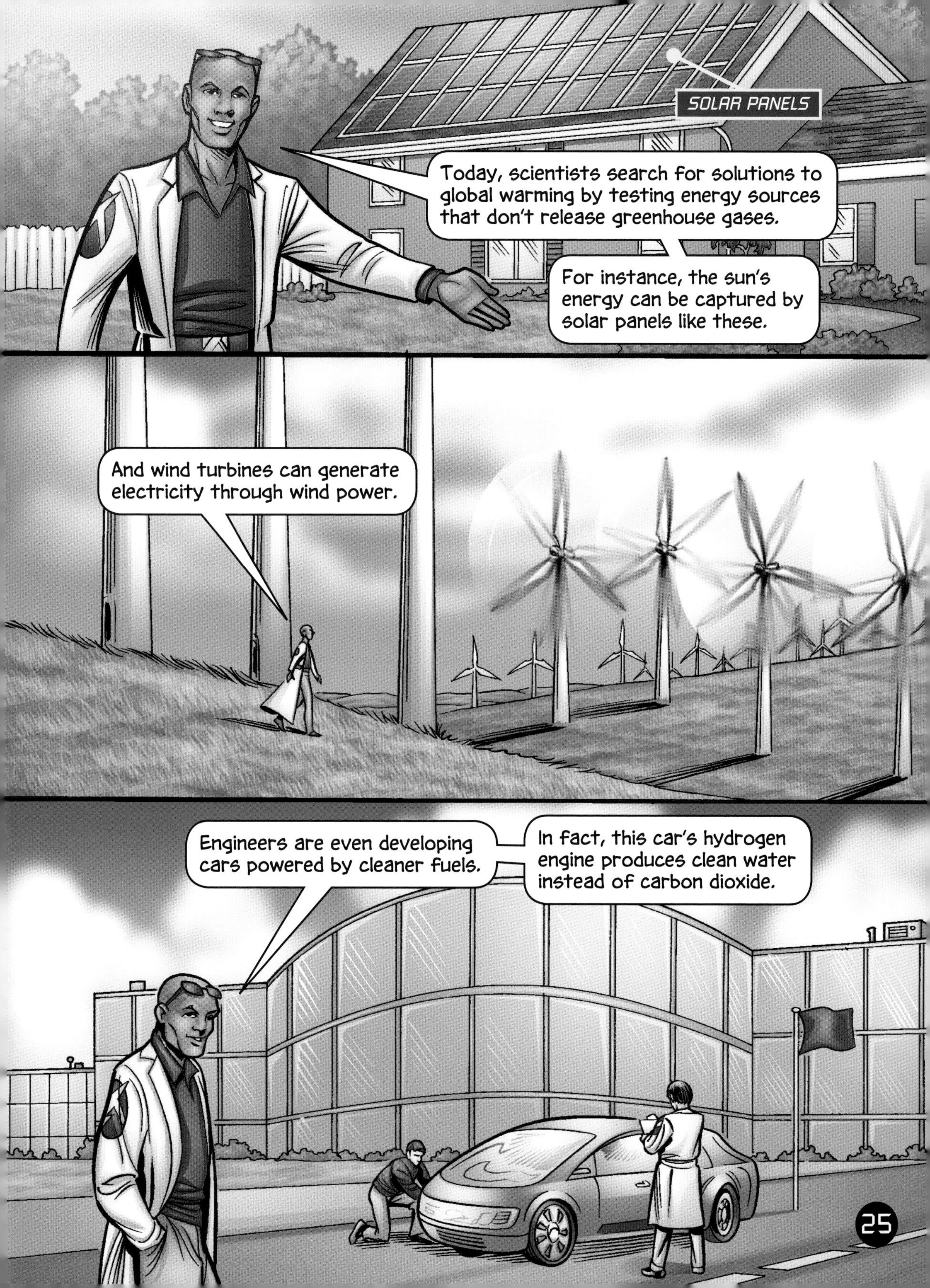
SOLAR PANELS
Today, scientists search for solutions to global warming by testing energy sources that don't release greenhouse gases.
For instance, the sun's energy can be captured by solar panels like these.
And wind turbines can generate electricity through wind power.
Engineers are even developing cars powered by cleaner fuels.
In fact, this car's hydrogen engine produces clean water instead of carbon dioxide.

MORE ABOUT GLOBAL WARMING

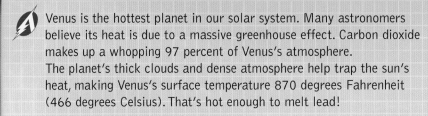

- Venus is the hottest planet in our solar system. Many astronomers believe its heat is due to a massive greenhouse effect. Carbon dioxide makes up a whopping 97 percent of Venus's atmosphere. The planet's thick clouds and dense atmosphere help trap the sun's heat, making Venus's surface temperature 870 degrees Fahrenheit (466 degrees Celsius). That's hot enough to melt lead!

- After carbon dioxide, methane is the greenhouse gas most produced by humans. Methane is released by landfills and is a by-product of coal mining. Believe it or not, cows are also a source of methane. When cows burp or pass gas, they release methane. As the demand for beef rises, more cattle are raised and more methane is released into the air.

- The United States is responsible for more greenhouse gas pollution than any other country in the world.

- Hurricanes have different names depending on where they occur in the world. If they appear on the Pacific Ocean, they're called typhoons. When they form on the Indian Ocean, they're called tropical cyclones.

- Ozone gas can be good or bad, depending on where it lies in the atmosphere. The ozone layer 10 to 30 miles (16 to 48 kilometers) high works as a shield to protect life on Earth from the sun's dangerous ultraviolet radiation. This radiation can lead to skin cancer in humans. Nearer the earth's surface, ground-level ozone is a health hazard, damaging lungs and hurting plants.

- The Arctic's sea ice is also melting quickly. Because snow and ice are white, the sea ice works like a big mirror, reflecting most of the sun's rays. As global temperatures rise, however, some of the ice melts. This melting reveals the ocean water below. Because the water is darker than the ice, it absorbs more of the sun's energy and warms up. The warmer water leads to even more of the sea ice melting, which leads to even more water being revealed. The cycle goes on and on.

- You've probably seen hybrid cars on the road or on TV. Hybrid cars run on both gasoline and electricity. Because they don't use as much gas as regular cars, they produce less pollution.

TEST THE WATERS

What happens to the world's oceans when sea—or land—ice begins to melt due to Earth's rising temperature? Build a simulation and find out!

WHAT YOU NEED:

- 2 empty and clean individual-serving yogurt containers
- water
- clean plastic paint pan
- sand or pebbles
- butter knife
- plastic ruler
- paper and pencil
- small cup

WHAT YOU DO:

1. Fill the yogurt containers with water and freeze overnight.

2. Cover the slope of the paint pan with sand or small pebbles. This section represents land.

3. Pour room-temperature water into the reservoir (the deep part) of the paint pan until it is about half full. This water represents the ocean.

4. Remove one yogurt container from the freezer. Use a butter knife to carefully remove the ice.

5. Add your ice to the reservoir. This ice represents sea ice.

6. Using the ruler, immediately measure how high the water comes up the side and slope of the paint pan. Record the measurements on a piece of paper.

7. On your paper, make a prediction about the water level. What do you think will happen when the ice melts?

8. When the ice is fully melted, use the ruler to measure the new water level. Record your measurements and compare them to your earlier measurements. What changed? Make any observations you notice.

9. Remove the second yogurt container from the freezer and take out the ice and place it on top of the sand or pebbles. This ice represents land ice, like a glacier.

10. On your paper, make a new prediction: what do you think will happen when the ice melts?

11. When the ice is fully melted, use the ruler to measure the new water level. Record your measurements and compare them to your first. What changed? Make any observations you notice.

DISCUSSION QUESTIONS

1. The use of fossil fuels contributes to global warming. How can people in your area reduce their use of fossil fuels to help slow down global warming?

2. What are at least five effects of global warming on our planet and its inhabitants? Which one do you think is the most harmful?

3. Discuss what you think will happen if temperatures continue to rise on Earth. Do you think rising temperatures are a good thing or a bad thing? Why?

4. How do changing temperatures have different effects on different people? Discuss who would be most strongly affected by heat waves and why.

WRITING PROMPTS

1. Humans have a major effect on global warming. List at least four human activities that contribute to Earth's greenhouse effect. Draw a picture to represent each activity.

2. What causes the thinning of Earth's ozone layer? Draw a diagram of the greenhouse effect.

3. Global warming can have effects even in your neighborhood. Write a paragraph explaining two effects global warming might have on your area.

4. Imagine it is the year 2100. Write a short news article explaining what effect global warming is having on Earth almost 100 years from now.

TAKE A QUIZ!

GLOSSARY

atmosphere (AT-muhs-fihr)—the mixture of gases that surrounds the earth

average (AV-uh-rij)—a common amount of something; an average amount is found by adding figures together and dividing by the number of figures.

carbon dioxide (KAHR-buhn dye-AHK-side)—a colorless, odorless gas that people and animals breathe out; plants take in carbon dioxide because they need it to live.

climate (KLEYE-mit)—the usual weather that occurs in a place

drought (DROUT)—a long period of weather with little or no rainfall

fossil fuels (FOSS-uhl FYOO-uhls)—natural fuels formed from the remains of plants and animals; coal, oil, and natural gas are fossil fuels.

glacier (GLAY-shur)—a huge moving body of ice found in mountain valleys or polar regions

habitat (HAB-uh-tat)—the natural place and conditions in which a plant or animal lives

ozone layer (OH-zohn LAY-ur)—the thin layer of ozone high above the earth's surface that blocks out some of the sun's harmful rays

photosynthesis (foh-toh-SIN-thuh-sis)—the process by which plant cells use energy from the sun to combine carbon dioxide, water, and minerals to make food for plant growth; photosynthesis releases oxygen into the atmosphere.

radiate (RAY-dee-ate)—to give off energy

READ MORE

Buchanan, Shelly. *Global Warming*. Science Readers: Content and Literacy Series. Huntington beach, Cali.: Teacher Created Materials, 2015.

Coutts, Lyn. *Global Warming*. Visual Explorers. Hauppauge, N.Y.: Barron's Educational Series, 2017.

Herman, Gail. *What is Climate Change?* What Was? Series. New York: Penguin Young Readers, an Imprint of Penguin Group Inc., 2018.

Mack, Molly. *Reducing Global Warming*. Global Guardians. New York: The Rosen Publishing Group, 2017.

INTERNET SITES

Use Facthound to find Internet sites related to this book.

Visit *www.facthound.com*

Just type in 9781543529531 and go!

 Check out projects, games and lots more at **www.capstonekids.com**

INDEX